Cupcakes for My Birthday

TEACHING COMPOUND WORDS

BY MARY LINDEEN

The Child's World®
childsworld.com

Published by The Child's World®
1980 Lookout Drive • Mankato, MN 56003-1705
800-599-READ • www.childsworld.com

ACKNOWLEDGMENTS
The Child's World®: Mary Swensen, Publishing Director
Red Line Editorial: Editorial direction and production
The Design Lab: Design

Photographs ©: Shutterstock Images, cover, 1, 2, 4, 5, 7, 12; Amee
Cross/Shutterstock Images, 6–7; Hatchapong Palurtchaivong/
Shutterstock Images, 8–9; iStockphoto, 10; Tatyana Vyc/
Shutterstock Images, 13; Oksana Trautwein/Shutterstock Images,
14; Mido Semsem/Shutterstock Images, 15

ISBN 9781503808355
LCCN 2015958432

Printed in the United States of America
Mankato, MN
June, 2016
PA02304

ABOUT THE AUTHOR
Mary Lindeen is a writer, editor, former
elementary school teacher, and parent. She
has written more than 100 books for children.
She specializes in early literacy instruction and
creating books for young readers.

A compound word is made by joining two or more words to make a bigger word with a new meaning. Look for **compound words** in this book. You will find them in **bold** type.

Sam eats **oatmeal** for **breakfast**.
Madison likes **buttermilk pancakes**.

Rudy plays **shortstop** on his **baseball** team. Ava plays **basketball** on the **playground**.

Drew does his **homework** in his **bedroom**.
Lauren takes her **notebook outside** to study.

Chris gets up before **daylight** to watch the **sunrise**.
Sofia stays up late to watch **fireflies** in the **moonlight**.

Sometimes Brett plays **barefoot** in the yard. Emma rides her **skateboard** on the **sidewalk** every **afternoon**.

Kai likes a **strawberry milkshake** with his **hamburger**.
I love to have **cupcakes** for my **birthday**!

Did you find these compound words?

afternoon	milkshake
barefoot	moonlight
baseball	notebook
basketball	oatmeal
bedroom	outside
birthday	pancakes
breakfast	playground
buttermilk	shortstop
cupcakes	sidewalk
daylight	skateboard
fireflies	sometimes
hamburger	strawberry
homework	sunrise

To Learn More

IN THE LIBRARY

Carle, Eric. *The Very Lonely Firefly*. New York: Penguin, 2012.

Hambleton, Laura, and Sedat Turhan. *Strawberry Bullfrog: Fun with Compound Words*. London: Milet, 2007.

Johnson-Bernardo, Le'Jon A. *BeeShu Butterfly: Compound Words*. Frederick, MD: America Star, 2011.

ON THE WEB

Visit our Web site for links about compound words:
childsworld.com/links

Note to Parents, Teachers, and Librarians: We routinely verify our Web links to make sure they are safe and active sites. So encourage your readers to check them out!